RAND NATIONAL DEFENSE RESEARCH INSTITUTE

Overcoming Challenges Arising from the Creation of National Security Councils

A Framework and Lessons from Sub-Saharan Africa

Arthur Chan

Prepared for the Office of the Secretary of Defense

For more information on this publication, visit www.rand.org/t/RR2694

Library of Congress Cataloging-in-Publication Data is available for this publication.
ISBN: 978-1-9774-0158-8

Published by the RAND Corporation, Santa Monica, Calif.
© Copyright 2018 RAND Corporation
RAND® is a registered trademark.

Support RAND
Make a tax-deductible charitable contribution at
www.rand.org/giving/contribute

www.rand.org

Preface

This report was written to aid in the work of the Comité de réflexion sur la coordination interministériel of the government of Mali as it looked into the possible establishment of a national security council. It looks particularly at what new challenges arise from the establishment of national security councils and how to effectively overcome such challenges. It examines the experiences in three countries in sub-Saharan Africa—Sierra Leone, Côte d'Ivoire, and Mozambique—in order to provide possible references to Mali.

This research was sponsored by the Center for Civil-Military Relations at the Naval Postgraduate School and conducted within the International Security and Defense Policy Center of the RAND National Defense Research Institute—a federally funded research and development center sponsored by the Office of the Secretary of Defense, the Joint Staff, the Unified Combatant Commands, the Navy, the Marine Corps, the defense agencies, and the defense Intelligence Community.

For more information on the RAND International Security and Defense Policy Center, see www.rand.org/nsrd/ndri/centers/isdp or contact the director (contact information is provided on the webpage).

Contents

Tables

Summary

This report examines what potential challenges arise as a result of setting up a national security council (NSC) and what the most effective means are for overcoming these challenges. The work is intended to serve as a reference to the government of Mali as it looks into establishing such a body for itself. Through a review of open source literature and interviews with subject-matter experts, this report creates a theoretical framework by which to measure the effectiveness of NSCs in terms of overcoming these potential challenges.

The report explains that the features that allow NSCs to most effectively overcome potential challenges fall into three overall categories: (1) defining roles and authority; (2) composition and accountability; and (3) ensuring sufficient resources. Each of these overall categories is composed of two or three variables. In terms of defining roles and authority, the two variables are whether there is a legislative or constitutional basis for the NSC and whether the NSC has the backing of the country's chief executive, be that individual the head of state or the head of government. In terms of composition and accountability, the three variables are whether the NSC is predominantly civilian in its composition but with relevant input from noncivilians; whether the NSC is appropriately sized, with virtually all of its members having responsibilities that directly touch upon national security; and whether there is accountability for the NSC. In terms of ensuring sufficient resources, the two variables are whether the NSC and its secretariat have appropriate levels of personnel and funding and whether the NSC has access to a broad range of expertise, be it from inside or outside of government. This creates a total of seven variables across three different categories.

Having established this framework, this report then applies it to three country case studies: Sierra Leone, Côte d'Ivoire, and Mozambique. These countries were selected because, like Mali, they are located in sub-Saharan Africa and have experienced internal conflict. This helps to control for "confounding variables" and makes their cases more relevant to the government of Mali. The report gives a brief overview of each country's internal conflicts and of the features of its NSC. It then gives each country a score for each of the seven variables. These scores are qualitative in nature and include "yes," "no," "mixed," and "information unavailable" for when the NSC could not be assessed. Sierra Leone's NSC received positive scores for all seven variables. Côte d'Ivoire's NSC received positive scores for three variables, a negative score for one, a mixed score for two, and could not be assessed for one. Finally, Mozambique's NSC received positive scores for four variables, a negative score for one, and mixed scores for the other two.

This assessment indicates that Sierra Leone has been most effective in overcoming the challenges that arise from the creation of a new NSC and therefore could be the best model for the government of Mali's efforts. The government of Mali could also follow a mixed model by taking the most-effective features from each of the three countries' NSCs and incorporating them into its own NSC.

However, an NSC that is effective at overcoming potential challenges and ultimately becoming a well-functioning body is not, itself, a cure-all for broader security environment challenges, such as ensuring either stability or effective implementation of security sector reforms. Other factors, such as the state of the economy and the status of former combatants, will also have a major impact on these broader challenges. It is therefore important that a government seeking to construct an effective, well-functioning NSC undertake such an action in conjunction with reforms elsewhere.

Acknowledgments

A number of people assisted with this report and made its publication possible. Michael Shurkin originally approached me with this topic and has been extremely supportive throughout the entire writing and review process. Equally important, he encouraged me to have this report published, and I would like to thank him for all his support. I would also like to thank the subject matter experts who very generously gave their time to speak with me and whose knowledge helped fill in a number of gaps in my research. Michael McNerney, King Mallory, and Puneet Talwar also provided excellent insights and suggestions. For that, I would like to thank them as well. Finally, I would like to thank Christine Wormuth, director of the International Security and Defense Policy Center; Andrew Parasiliti, director of the RAND Center for Global Risk and Security; and Caroline Baxter, the project's co-lead, for their support.

Abbreviations

CISU	Central Intelligence and Security Unit
CNDS	Conselho Nacional de Defesa e Segurança (National Council of Defense and Security)
DCAF	Geneva Centre for the Democratic Control of Armed Forces
DISEC	district security committee
FRELIMO	Frente de Libertação de Moçambique (Mozambique Liberation Front)
JIC	Joint Intelligence Committee
NaScia	The National Security and Central Intelligence Act, 2002
NSC	national security council
ONS	Office of National Security
ONSC	Office of the National Security Council
PROSEC	provincial security committee
RENAMO	Resistência Nacional Moçambicana (Mozambican National Resistance)
RFI	Radio France Internationale
SSR	security sector reform
UNAMSIL	United Nations Mission in Sierra Leone
UNOCI	United Nations Operation in Côte d'Ivoire

CHAPTER ONE

Introduction

This report examines what potential challenges arise from the establishment of a national security council (NSC) and what elements are needed in order to effectively overcome such challenges. Its approach to doing so consists of two parts: (1) a review of previous literature and open sources so as to establish a theoretical framework by which to measure effectiveness in overcoming such challenges and (2) a selection of three case studies to which to apply the framework. In adopting this approach, the report's objective is to provide both theoretical reference and concrete examples that the government of Mali will be able to use as it looks into establishing its own NSC.

The rest of the report is organized as follows: the first section of Chapter One presents an overview of NSCs. It is divided into two parts: the first part looks at what the reasons and benefits are for establishing an NSC, while the second part looks at what potential new challenges arise from doing so. The second section of Chapter One describes the methodology of this report. It begins by providing an overview of the types of sources used to build the report's theoretical framework and then moves on to explain the criteria used to select the countries for case study. Chapter Two describes the theoretical framework in depth. It compares a range of sources to see what are the most commonly cited measures of national security council "effectiveness" but then matches up these measures to the potential challenges discussed in Chapter One to see how policymakers might overcome these challenges. Afterward, it pulls all of these elements together in order to establish a framework to apply to the case studies. Chapters Three, Four, and Five are the case studies, focusing respectively on Sierra Leone, Côte d'Ivoire, and Mozambique. Each of these chapters in turn is composed of three subsections that examine (1) the security and political situation of the country leading up to the establishment of its NSC, (2) a description of the institutional features of its NSC, and (3) an application of the framework to the case study. Chapter Six concludes the report, summarizing the previous chapters' findings and then providing suggestions on how Mali could possibly apply these lessons to its own situation and overcome potential challenges that may arise from establishing an NSC.

Overview of National Security Council

Reasons for Establishing a National Security Council

The reasons why a government may choose to establish an NSC vary but usually have to do with improving the quality of national security decisionmaking. An NSC serves as a formal body bringing together all the relevant government agencies with a role in the security sector, thereby allowing them to better coordinate their actions. This is particularly important in situations where different agencies may have overlapping responsibilities or where the government must respond to national security challenges that do not fall neatly into any one agency's area of competence. Insurgencies and wars—particularly civil wars—are examples of these kinds of challenges. They usually require the effort of some combination of the military, the police, the gendarmerie, intelligence agencies, and the diplomatic service to address the matter. In such a situation, it is necessary to have some kind of institutional mechanism for bringing together the principals of these different agencies in order to de-conflict their actions and prevent them from working at cross-purposes. Otherwise, coordination would become subject to the discretion of individual personalities, which would lead to a lack of continuity as people rotate in and out of offices. For example, this was one of the reasons behind the establishment of the U.S. National Security Council as part of a more general reorganization of the country's national security apparatus: "Proponents of the reform realized that no institutional means for the coordination of foreign and defense policy existed, and that the informal management techniques employed by President Roosevelt . . . and President Truman . . . were not suitable for the long haul."[1]

Potential New Challenges in Establishing a National Security Council

In spite of the potential for improving coordination and, in turn, the quality of national security decisionmaking, the establishment of an NSC may lead to a number of potential new challenges as well. These potential challenges fall into the three following overall categories:

1. The NSC may gradually usurp the authority of other executive agencies such as the defense or foreign ministries, or it may otherwise interfere with their decisions. This is a particular possibility as the NSC grows larger and more well funded—perhaps to the point where its principals feel the temptation to insert themselves into the actions of other agencies. In such a scenario, the NSC transforms into an additional layer of bureaucracy, thereby slowing down decisionmaking and possibly reducing its quality as well.

2. The NSC becomes a tool for authoritarian consolidation. This is particularly likely if the NSC ends up usurping the authority of the government ministries and has the intelligence services reporting directly to it. In such a scenario, the NSC concentrates power over the security forces and becomes a sort of "supreme command." Whether such a scenario can be prevented depends to a large extent on political will, both on part of the executive branch to accept oversight and on part of the legislative branch to exercise it. If the legislative branch lacks the will or even the capacity to exercise oversight, and if the executive branch is determined to use the NSC in a partisan fashion, then the likelihood it will become a tool for authoritarian consolidation

---

[1]   U.S. Department of State, Office of the Historian, "History of the National Security Council, 1947–1997," *The Clinton White House Archives*, August 1997.

increases. When the NSC is *not* primarily comprised of civilians but is instead a military-heavy body, this danger also increases.

3. The NSC may absorb or steal resources from other executive agencies, particularly in terms of talent and funding. The NSC may, for example, "poach" talent from other agencies. An increasingly important NSC may also require an increased budget, with resources being diverted from the budgets of other agencies. These resources, moreover, may not always be wisely used. Policymakers may, for example, deliberately try to expand the NSC through mass hiring of new personnel, prioritizing quantity over quality.

In all of these scenarios, there may be bureaucratic pushback from other government agencies. Actors in places such as the defense, interior, and foreign ministries may resent the growing influence of the NSC, leading to "turf wars." This could lead to bureaucratic paralysis. Otherwise, one side or the other might ultimately "win" the confrontation, and the NSC may grow more powerful but at the expense of hollowing out other agencies, or the agencies may succeed in sidelining the NSC. Each of these outcomes, however, is undesirable and may lead to a decline in the quality of national security decisionmaking in one way or another. The goal of policymakers when establishing an NSC should be to avoid such outcomes and, as much as is possible, overcome the abovementioned challenges.

Methodology

Sources

One of the major challenges for this report was finding the right sources from which to draw in order to build the theoretical framework for assessing how effective NSCs are in overcoming the various categories of potential challenges. There is no single model for NSCs, and individual councils may vary dramatically from one to another as a function of their environments. The U.S. National Security Council, for example, differs from the National Security Commission of the Chinese Communist Party or the Supreme National Security Council of Iran or even the National Defense and Security Council of France in terms of its intended role/functions and actual activities. Because of these differences, there are few systematic studies of NSCs as a general subject and none of substantial length on which this report can draw.

This report therefore makes use of general studies on NSCs where available. At the same time, it also draws on the following four additional types of sources to help build its theoretical framework:

1. studies on the NSCs of individual countries. There are a number of such studies that offer particular insight into how individual NSCs function as well as critiques on where they might improve in their functioning

2. studies on security sector reforms (SSR), which often have components that deal with building or strengthening national security decisionmaking structures. Such studies will make detailed recommendations on how best to organize top-level structures such as NSCs in order to best implement SSR

3. studies on SSR for individual countries. These studies also often have components dealing with NSCs, either in terms of how to set them up or how to improve the functioning of preexisting ones

4. interviews with subject matter experts. After examining the critiques and recommendations presented by these sources, this report pulls together all these elements in order to create a framework for assessing the NSCs presented in the case studies in terms of how effective they have been at overcoming the categories of potential challenges.

Selection of Countries for Case Studies

The selection of countries for case studies was based primarily on two criteria—relevance and availability of information. In terms of the first criterion, this report's aim is to choose countries whose experiences have been most similar to Mali's while also controlling for "confounding variables" as much as possible. The second criterion, meanwhile, very much functioned as a limitation as well. Because detailed information regarding the setup and activities of NSCs is not always publicly available, that necessarily reduced the number of potential choices for case studies to just those NSCs that had the most information available about them—although even then, there were certain gaps.

Using these two criteria, this report surveyed a range of developed and developing countries in different regions of the world before ultimately deciding on three: Sierra Leone, Côte d'Ivoire, and Mozambique. All three are sub-Saharan African states, with the first two also located in West Africa and the latter located in Southeast Africa. Like Mali, all three countries have also experienced significant periods of political and security instability. In the case of Sierra Leone, this was the civil war of 1991–2002. In the case of Côte d'Ivoire, this includes the 2002–2007 civil war as well as the shorter civil war of 2010–2011, which followed the 2010 presidential election. Finally, in the case of Mozambique, this includes the war of independence from Portugal (1964–1974), the civil war (1977–1992), and, more recently, the ongoing low-level conflict between the government and opposition (2013–present). These three countries also set up their NSCs in the aftermath of their periods of instability, often with the explicit aim of carrying out security sector reforms and consolidating peace.

The similarity of their experiences and geopolitical situations make these three countries especially significant for Mali. Moreover, Mali's geographical proximity to these countries—and in particular with Sierra Leone and Côte d'Ivoire, both West African states—may make it easier to do outreach to government counterparts for lessons learned. Finally, there is sufficient availability of information regarding these three countries' NSCs and the political and security environments in which they operate.

CHAPTER TWO

Theoretical Framework for Assessing National Security Council Effectiveness in Overcoming Challenges

As previous studies have noted, there is no "one size fits all" approach when it comes to NSCs.[1] A common thread running through NSCs is that "their role is always to bring the disparate parts of the security agenda together," but beyond that there is great variation, in practice, in what they are actually called on to do.[2] Measuring the general effectiveness of an NSC, then, is to a large extent a function of the intentions of the individual government. That being said, a review of different sources shows that there is large congruence among researchers on what are the essential features that NSCs must have in order to be effective. These essential features may be grouped into three overall categories: defining the roles and authority of the NSC; establishing a balanced composition while also holding the NSC accountable; and ensuring adequate resources for the NSC. Each of these three main categories, in turn, corresponds roughly with each of the three categories of potential challenges described in Chapter One. Specifically defining the roles and authority of the NSC responds to the potential challenge of the NSC's gradually usurping the authority of other government agencies. Making sure that the NSC has a predominantly

---

[1] Susanna Bearne, Olga Oliker, Kevin A. O'Brien, and Andrew Rathmell, *National Security Decision-Making Structures and Security Sector Reform*, Santa Monica, Calif.: RAND Corporation, TR-289-SSDAT, 2005, p. 29.

[2] Bearne et al., 2005, p. 2.

civilian composition and is politically accountable counteracts the potential challenge of the NSC's becoming a tool for authoritarian consolidation. Finally, ensuring that the NSC has access to adequate resources responds to the potential challenge of the NSC's absorbing or stealing resources from other agencies. Having these essential features, then, helps an NSC to overcome these three categories of potential challenges.

Overcoming Challenge 1: Defining Roles and Authority

NSCs may be called on to perform a variety of roles, including (1) providing forums in which to discuss joint assessments, to decide on courses of action, and to agree on responsibilities; (2) advising decisionmakers on resource allocation issues; (3) exercising oversight in the security sector; (4) providing expertise and advice to decisionmakers on security priorities; (5) carrying out emergency coordination; and (6) defining the direction and scope of security sector reform.[3] Depending on the government as well, an NSC may be either a purely advisory body or one with decisionmaking powers. Whatever the specific roles an NSC is called on to play, however, they should be clearly defined. The NSC must also have clearly defined authority to carry out actions associated with these roles. If an NSC's roles and authority are not clearly defined, then it will be difficult for both its members and outsiders to know the exact extent of its responsibilities along with where it is or is not actually competent to act. This has the potential to give rise to the first challenge that comes from establishing an NSC. Ill-defined limits to its authority may lead to overreach by the NSC wherein it usurps the authority of other executive agencies or otherwise actively interferes with their functioning. In this way, the NSC, rather than being a coordinating body, transforms into an additional layer of bureaucracy, thereby further slowing down the work of government. In the opposite case, the NSC may encounter pushback and ultimately be sidelined by other major actors within the security sector, such as the Ministry of Defense or the intelligence community, or even by ad hoc bodies created by the executive. The key, then, is to establish a balance whereby the NSC not only does not interfere or usurp but also is not a hollow institution.

---

[3] Bearne et al., 2005, pp. 2–4.

One means of clearly defining and circumscribing an NSC's responsibilities while also bolstering its authority is through official legislation. One study notes, for example, that "for an NSC to have legitimacy, it should have a legislative basis and high-level support."[4] Another piece, arguing for a redesign of Nepal's NSC, asserts that "in order to foster legitimacy, Nepal's new NSC should be authorized from parliamentary legislation and broad constitutional provisions, not merely by statute."[5] Other studies on Palestinian security sector reforms have also noted the Palestinian National Security Council's lack of a legislative basis as a major shortcoming, with one analyst recommending in 2007 that the Basic Law be amended again "to give the NSC a sound constitutional basis and to define its relationship with the Cabinet."[6] The NSC, then, should have a legal basis in order to provide it with the legitimacy it needs to act. This legal basis can either be through regular legislation or, as some countries have done, through incorporation of the NSC into the constitution.

The authority of an NSC may further be bolstered through active backing from the country's chief executive. Under a parliamentary system, this would be the head of government—the prime minister. Under a presidential or semipresidential system, this would be the head of state—the president. In the case of Nepal, one analyst argued that the National Security Council, which was previously under the Ministry of Defense, should be placed directly under the Office of the Prime Minister to provide it with support from the highest level decisionmaker.[7] Another study argued that, in the case of Liberia, the NSC should be "chaired by the President as commander in chief" and

---

[4] Bearne et al., 2005, p. 22.

[5] Madhav Ghimire, "A Case for Redesigning Nepal's National Security Council," *Foreign Policy*, August 13, 2014.

[6] Asem Khalil, "The Legal Framework for Palestinian Security Sector Governance" in Roland Friedrich and Arnold Luethold, eds., *Entry-Points for Palestinian Security Sector Reform*, Geneva.: Geneva Centre for the Democratic Control of Armed Forces (DCAF), 2007, p. 40; Palestinian Academic Society for the Study of International Affairs (PASSIA) and DCAF, "Security Sector Reform in the Palestinian Territories: Challenges and Prospects, Workshop Summary Report" in PASSIA and DCAF, eds., *Palestinian Security Sector Governance: Challenges and Prospects*, Jerusalem and Geneva, August, 2006, p. 23.

[7] Ghimire, 2014.

have "final authority over all security forces."[8] In the case of Zimbabwe, a Human Rights Watch report noted that the "National Security Council (NSC) has not had any impact on Zimbabwe's security sector as the body has remained dysfunctional owing to infrequent meetings," with President Robert Mugabe preferring to instead meet and discuss security issues with the heads of the security forces as part of the Joint Operations Command (JOC).[9] For an NSC to be effective, as such, the chief executive of the country must actively back it and participate in its operations. The chief executive must convene the NSC regularly and use it as the primary forum for cross-government discussions of major security issues. On the flip side, the NSC—namely, the NSC staff/secretariat—can gain the support of the chief executive by showing themselves to be competent and trusted to provide high-quality support, no matter which party might be in power.

Overcoming Challenge 2: Establishing a Balanced Composition and Accountability

NSCs, by their nature, are meant to be whole-of-government bodies that examine security issues beyond a narrowly military perspective. They are intended to handle both traditional and nontraditional security issues, looking at things that are normally beyond the remit of what bodies like the ministry of defense or the intelligence community handle. Because of this, in order to be effective, an NSC must have a balanced composition that draws its members from across government and from both the civilian and military/intelligence sectors. If the NSC is composed strictly of civilians, then it risks cutting itself off from the valuable expert input needed for decisionmaking. If, on the other hand, the NSC's composition tilts more heavily toward military/intelligence personnel, then that risks undermining civilian control of the military and security agencies. This leads to the second potential challenge in establishing an NSC, whereby it becomes a tool for authoritarian con-

---

[8]   David C. Gompert, Olga Oliker, Brooke Stearns, Keith Crane, and K. Jack Riley, *Making Liberia Safe: Transformation of the National Security Sector*, Santa Monica, Calif.: RAND Corporation, MG-529-OSD, 2007, p. 64.

[9]   Human Rights Watch, *The Elephant in the Room: Reforming Zimbabwe's Security Sector Ahead of Elections*, New York: Human Rights Watch, June 4, 2013.

solidation, concentrating control over all the security and intelligence forces of the country in the hands of just a few individuals or even just one sole individual—the chief executive of the country. Although authoritarian control is possible even when the body is predominantly civilian in composition, it is even likelier when its members are drawn primarily from the military and security services. The NSC in such a situation ends up shutting out civilians and transforms into a sort of military "high command." An example of this is the National Security Council of Turkey (*Milli Güvenlik Kurulu*), which was historically dominated by the country's military and served as vehicle through which it influenced national policies. As one study notes, "It is critical for NSCs to have a balance between military and civilian influence. Intelligence and security services must also be integrated effectively to support effective decision-making."[10] Yet another study argues, "It is critical for an NSC to have an appropriate balance between civilians and uniformed actors with clear mechanisms for civilian control."[11] An appropriate balance, then, might be one where the NSC is predominantly composed of civilians but also has relevant input from noncivilians.

At a minimum, then, the NSC should have the chief executive (president or prime minister) as its chair and include the key ministers handling security-related issues, such as those of defense, foreign affairs, and the interior. It should further include the heads of security agencies, such as the intelligence community, the police, and the military. A study on Liberia, for example, recommended that a Liberian NSC "should be chaired by the President and should include at its core the Ministers of Justice, Defense, Finance, and Foreign Affairs. It should receive professional advice and objective analysis from the head of national intelligence, the most senior officers of the LNP [Liberian National Police] and AFL [Armed Forces of Libya], and from the Liberian National Security Advisor."[12]

The need for it to be inclusive notwithstanding, the NSC must also be a nimble enough to provide timely advice and, if necessary, react

---

[10] Bearne et al., 2005, p. 26.

[11] DCAF, "National Security Councils (and Related Bodies)," *DCAF Backgrounder* 11/2010, Geneva, November 2010, pp. 5–6.

[12] Gompert et al., 2007, p. 76.

to contingencies. That is, while including as broad a range of expertise as possible allows the NSC to be more informed, such a variety also runs the risk of making it too big or even bloated. The composition of the NSC, then, must be rightsized. It must have at its core a statutory number of members who are needed to provide input on a broad range of security issues, but not be so big and include so many superfluous members that it essentially replicates the workings of the cabinet. Noncore members and other experts, meanwhile, could be invited to attend meetings on an ad hoc basis and with none of the rights that the core members of the NSC have. Ultimately, the NSC must be appropriately sized, where virtually all of its members have national security responsibilities.

In order to further guard against the NSC becoming an instrument for authoritarian consolidation, policymakers—lawmakers, in particular—may look into some mechanisms for holding the body accountable. The primary question, however, is how accountability may be exercised in practice, as NSCs are usually not set up as responsible bodies in the same sense as cabinets are in parliamentary systems. However, if the NSC is established formally through either legislative or constitutional means, then at the time of its creation, the legislature may inscribe certain limitations to its authority in order to prevent overreach. This would additionally help contribute to overcoming the first challenge of the NSC's usurping the authority of other agencies. The NSC may, for example, be obliged to consult with the legislature in matters such as the domestic use of military force.[13] NSC personnel, such as the national security adviser, may also be subject to parliamentary approval before being appointed to their posts, while the NSC and/or its subcomponents might be legally obliged to present annual reports on its activities to parliament. Otherwise, accountability may also be obtainable through indirect means, such as holding the government and individual ministers accountable for their policies. Another method might be to set up a legal affairs office within the NSC. The U.S. Legal Office of the NSC, for example, "provides advice and assistance to the President [on] the interpretation of U.S. domestic law, international treaties, and customary international law arising in the

---

[13] Gompert et al., 2007, p. 77.

consideration of national security issues."[14] A strong legal affairs office would help to interpret and vet potential acts of the NSC to make sure that they conform to both domestic and international laws, thereby preventing overreach and abuse of power.[15] All this having been said, however, whether or not an NSC can be held accountable depends to a great degree on political will. It depends considerably on whether lawmakers have the will and the capacity to hold the government and on whether the government is willing to be held accountable and not use the NSC as a partisan tool against political opponents.

Overcoming Challenge 3: Ensuring Sufficient Resources

The final and crucial component to an effective NSC is that it—and its secretariat—must have sufficient resources to perform their roles correctly. Such resources may be material, such as appropriate levels and stable sources of personnel and funding. They may also be nonmaterial, such as access to both the breadth and depth of expertise needed to inform discussions and/or decisionmaking. Indeed, one study cites both adequate resources and sufficient expertise as preconditions for an NSC to be effective. In particular:

- **Adequate resources.** When an NSC lacks personnel and financial resources, its deliberations can end up being infrequent; when they do take place they are likely to be poorly prepared and their overall usefulness suffers, with the result that informal consultations tend to take over.
- **Sufficient expertise.** Even where resources are available, NSCs may suffer from a lack of expertise for dealing with security issues. New and postconflict countries can be particularly disadvantaged in this respect: new countries because there is little or no tradition in this area, postconflict countries because elites may have been decimated or discredited during the conflict, or may have relocated in its wake.[16]

---

[14] Clinton White House Archives, "National Security Council. Legal Advisor: Special Assistant to the President and Legal Advisor," n.d.

[15] Interview with subject matter expert, July 13, 2018.

[16] DCAF, 2010, p. 5.

The two previous criteria for measuring NSC effectiveness in responding to potential challenges—authority and composition—feed into the third criteria of sufficient resources in certain ways. If the chief executive wishes to enhance the NSC's authority, he or she may find ways of increasing the material resources available to the NSC to help it carry out its functions. Meanwhile, having the right composition of ministers and other leaders from across the government provides the NSC with at least a base level of broad expertise to inform its discussions. However, an NSC should not limit itself to just expertise at the top of government. It must go below the ministerial level and also draw in outside experts. In the case of Liberia, for example, a RAND study in 2007 suggested that "from subcabinet to working levels, interagency communication, including the participation of the armed and intelligence services, must be a way of life in the Liberian security sector" and that "legal and substantial experts from Liberia and its partners should be engaged to frame a new national security law under the direction of the NSC."[17] An NSC, as such, should draw on nonmaterial resources both horizontally and vertically. That is, it should reach across government to draw on expertise available in other national-level agencies but also reach down and draw on expertise available in subnational agencies and even from academia and the private sector.

Another means to ensure that the NSC has sufficient material and nonmaterial resources is to make sure that it has subordinate agencies—such as a secretariat—for carrying out its will, and that these agencies, in turn, also have sufficient resources. Without subordinate agencies, the NSC essentially becomes a talking shop with no actual coordination function. An NSC secretariat is particularly important here, as it is the main arm of the NSC. Depending on the specific role envisioned for this secretariat, it may variously be called on to act as coordinator, implementer, and/or in-house think tank. These roles may also shift over time: in postconflict environments, the secretariat may be called on to do more and manage more complex processes. As conditions improve, however, the country's chief executive may wish for the secretariat to play a smaller, less active role and to relinquish its responsibilities to other institutions as the latter become

---

[17] Gompert et al., 2007, pp. 46, 79.

stronger. The chief executive may also not necessarily wish to reduce the secretariat's role but merely shift it to have it focus on other issues. Whatever the case, secretariats must have levels of resources appropriate to any and all of the roles it is called on to play and to support the NSC to do *its* job in turn. The case of Afghanistan's Office of the National Security Council (ONSC) is illustrative of the importance of having a well-resourced secretariat. In spite of initial pretensions by certain high-level members of the ONSC to actually being the NSC itself, the ONSC was eventually sidelined by "much more powerful, well-funded and well-supported rivals in the security sector, chiefly the MoD [Ministry of Defense] and Interior and the NDS [National Directorate of Security]."[18] The ONSC needed more resources in order to establish its legitimacy, including "a sufficient number of capable and dedicated staff members to produce a quality product and to draft security policy and security strategy, thereby earning . . . acceptance elsewhere in government and eventually in the provinces."[19]

However, although the secretariat (and other agencies subordinate to the NSC) must have sufficient resources to do their jobs and to support the NSC, there also needs to be a balance. As with deciding on composition, there is also an issue of rightsizing when it comes to allocating resources. This is the third challenge that comes from establishing an NSC, whereby the newly created body absorbs/steals resources—particularly talent and funding—from other agencies. In order to overcome this challenge, policymakers must be careful when it comes to allocating resources to the NSC. Too few resources and the NSC cannot do its job. Meanwhile, too many resources risks creating another layer of bureaucracy. It further increases the temptation of the NSC, its secretariat, and other subordinate agencies to actively intervene in the workings of other parts of government or to appropriate those functions for themselves, leading back to the first challenge. In the context of U.S. politics, this has led to situations where the NSC is overly operational rather than focused on strategic issues. To remedy

---

[18] Christian Dennys and Tom Hamilton-Baillie, *Strategic Support to Security Sector Reform in Afghanistan, 2001–2010*, SSR Issue Papers No. 6, Waterloo, Ont.: The Centre for International Governance Innovation, January 2012, pp. 9–10.

[19] Dennys and Hamilton-Baillie, 2012, p. 13.

Table 2.1
Theoretical Framework for Assessing National Security Council's Effectiveness in Overcoming Challenges

Category	Variable	Level in Present Case
Defining roles and authority	Is there a legislative or constitutional basis for the NSC?	
	Does the NSC have the backing of the country's chief executive (head of state or head of government)?	
Composition and accountability	Is the NSC predominantly civilian but with relevant input from noncivilians?	
	Is the NSC appropriately-sized, with virtually all NSC members having national security responsibilities?	
	Is there accountability for the NSC?	
Ensuring sufficient resources	Does the NSC and its secretariat have appropriate levels of personnel and funding?	
	Does the NSC have access to a broad range of expertise?	

this, certain experts have recommended reducing the size of the NSC staff, particularly in terms of its middle management: "a thinner layer of middle management would help curb the impulse for the NSC to become too operational."[20] Such an approach would work for other NSC secretariats as well, ensuring that they have sufficient resources but not so much that they set themselves up as a parallel government. An adequate level of resources helps to overcome not only the third challenge but the first one as well.

Taking what was discussed previously, this report establishes a theoretical framework (Table 2.1) for measuring how effectively NSCs are in overcoming potential challenges. It is divided into three categories, each composed of several variables. In the case studies, each country's NSC is assessed within this framework. The NSC is given an assessment of "yes," "no," "mixed," and "information unavailable" against each of the variables.

---

[20] Charles P. Ries, *Improving Decisionmaking in a Turbulent World*, Santa Monica, Calif.: RAND Corporation, PE-129-RC, 2016, p. 34.

CHAPTER THREE

Case Study 1: Sierra Leone

Political Situation of Sierra Leone

Sierra Leone's most significant period of upheaval in the postwar period was its civil war, which lasted from 1991 to 2002. Prior to that, the country had become independent in 1961, experienced two military coups in 1967 and 1968, and became a one-party state in 1978.[1]

The civil war began in 1991 when "former army corporal Foday Sankoh and his Revolutionary United Front (RUF) began to campaign against President Momoh."[2] In July 1999, the government and rebels signed a peace agreement after six weeks of talks in the Togolese capital of Lomé; in November/December of the same year, the United Nations deployed to Sierra Leone under the United Nations Mission in Sierra Leone (UNAMSIL) in order to police the agreement.[3] At its maximum deployment in March 2002, UNAMSIL had 17,368 military personnel, contributed by 28 countries.[4] Sporadic conflict continued until January 2002, when the war was declared over, with UNAMSIL saying that disarmament of 45,000 fighters was complete.[5] The conflict was

---

[1] "Sierra Leone Profile—Timeline," *BBC News*, July 13, 2017.

[2] "Sierra Leone Profile—Timeline," 2017.

[3] "Sierra Leone Profile—Timeline," 2017.

[4] UNAMSIL, "Sierra Leone—UNAMSIL—Facts and Figures," in *The Wayback Machine*, September 12, 2008.

[5] "Sierra Leone Profile—Timeline," 2017.

particularly known for its brutality; casualties were estimated to be between 30,000 and 50,000, and possibly as high as 70,000, with 2.6 million displaced people.[6]

Sierra Leone's National Security Council

Sierra Leone's National Security Council was established via "The National Security and Central Intelligence Act, 2002" (SCIA) following the end of its civil war and as part of the SSRs that then began to take place. According to the NaSCIA, the NSC's standing members include the president, as chairman; the vice president, as deputy chairman; the ministers of finance, foreign affairs, internal affairs, and information and broadcasting; the deputy minister of defense; the minister of state for presidential affairs; the inspector-general of police; the chief of defense staff; and the national security coordinator, who also doubles as the NSC's secretary. In addition, the "President may, after consultation with the Council, invite such person, as he considers necessary for any deliberations of the Council," although the invitees do not have any voting rights.[7] It should further be noted that as of 2016, the position of minister of state for presidential affairs no longer exists, meaning that the NSC may now consist of just ten core members.[8]

The NaSCIA states that the "Object for which the Council is established is to provide highest forum for the consideration and determination of matters relating to the security of Sierra Leone" and, to that end, has responsibilities in seven overall areas. These include (1) considering and taking "appropriate measures to safeguard the internal and external security of Sierra Leone"; (2) ensuring "the gathering of information relating to the security of Sierra Leone and the integra-

---

[6] World Peace Foundation, "Sierra Leone," *Mass Atrocity Endings*, August 7, 2015b; Mary Kaldor, with James Vincent, *Case Study Sierra Leone: Evaluation of UNDP Assistance to Conflict-Affected Countries*, New York: United Nations Development Programme Evaluation Office, 2006, p. 4.

[7] "The National Security and Central Intelligence Act, 2002," *Supplement to the Sierre Leone Gazette*, Vol. CXXXII, No. 42, July 4, 2002.

[8] Peter Andersen, "President Koroma's Fifth Cabinet: 13 March 2016 to 27 March 2018," *The Sierra Leone Web*, 2018.

tion of domestic and foreign security policies"; (3) directing the operations of the Joint Intelligence Committee, the provincial and district security committees, and the Central Intelligence and Security Unit; (4) approving "any major plans and recommendations by the Ministry responsible for defence"; (5) monitoring "all external military support to Sierra Leone"; (6) acting "as a War Cabinet as and when required"; and (7) "to do all such things as will contribute to the attainment of the object of the Council."[9]

The NSC in addition has a series of structures to support its activities at both the national and subnational level. In the former case, the NSC has at its disposal the Central Intelligence and Security Unit (CISU), which—as its name suggests—is responsible for intelligence collection and security matters and which must present an annual report to parliament on its operations.[10] Also supporting the NSC is the Office of National Security (ONS), led by the National Security Coordinator, whom the president appoints subject to the approval of parliament. The National Security Coordinator acts as principal adviser to the president and government on security issues, providing support/ secretarial services to the NSC, chairing the Joint Intelligence Committee (JIC), and coordinating on security and disaster response issues at both the national and subnational level.[11] The National Security Coordinator further chairs the NSC Coordinating Group (NSCCG).

> The JIC is a forum for the intelligence community to consider and endorse intelligence assessments provided by the ONS joint assessment team (JAT). The NSCCG includes the heads of security sector institutions and senior civil servants of relevant line ministries. It provides specific guidance in the implementation of NSC directives. The collaborative work of these bodies fosters cooperation and keeps individual security institutions fully aware of the overall direction of activities.[12]

---

[9] "The National Security and Central Intelligence Act, 2002," p. 4.

[10] "The National Security and Central Intelligence Act, 2002," pp. 7–9.

[11] "The National Security and Central Intelligence Act, 2002," p. 10.

[12] Kellie Hassan Conteh, "Security Sector Reform in Sierra Leone and the Role of the Office of National Security," in Peter Albrecht and Paul Jackson, eds., *Security Sector Reform in*

The ONS serves as the secretariat of the NSC. It consists of somewhere between 150 and 200 staff members.[13] For comparison, the U.S. National Security Council staff approached nearly 400 in mid-2016.[14] France's Sécretariat Général de la Défense et de la Sécurité Nationale, meanwhile, had 896 staff in 2015, which subsequently grew to 972 in 2016.[15] Within the domestic context, Sierra Leone's most recent *Defence White Paper* indicates that the Ministry of Defense employed about 165 people circa 2003.[16] This makes the ONS appear to be a relatively large body, both when compared to other domestic agencies and to international counterparts. On the other hand, when compared to the range of responsibilities that the ONS has—which includes coordinating on serious organized crime, border security, and other security issues—even a staff of 150–200 people appears insufficient. According to one subject matter expert, at the time of the ONS's creation, the Sierra Leonean government and its British advisers decided to make the body relatively small but with a high level of expertise, allowing ONS staff to effectively analyze intelligence and advise the government.[17] Individuals may apply directly to the ONS for positions and are subject to a vetting process in order to ensure their political neutrality as well as the neutrality of the ONS as a whole.[18] This aspect of the ONS has historically been a double-edged sword for the body: while the ONS has managed to maintain its political neutrality, this has also made successive presidents not

---

Sierra Leone 1997–2007: Views from the Front Line, Geneva: Geneva Centre for the Democratic Control of Armed Forces, 2010, p. 177.

[13] Interview with subject matter expert, January 22, 2018.

[14] Mark F. Cancian, "Limiting the Size of NSC Staff," Washington, D.C.: Center for Strategic and International Studies, July 1, 2016, p. 1.

[15] Sécretariat Général de la Défense et de la Sécurité Nationale, *Rapport d'Activité 2015* [*Activity Report 2015*], Paris, France: Sécretariat Général de la Défense et de la Sécurité Nationale, 2015, p. 6; Sécretariat Général de la Défense et de la Sécurité Nationale, *Rapport d'Activité 2016* [*Activity Report 2016*], Paris, France: Sécretariat Général de la Défense et de la Sécurité Nationale, 2016, p. 7.

[16] Sierra Leone Government, *Defence White Paper: Informing the People*, Freetown, SL: Directorate of Defence Policy, Ministry of Defence, 2003, p. 14.

[17] Interview with subject matter expert, January 19, 2018.

[18] Interview with subject matter expert, January 19, 2018.

entirely trust the ONS because the body is not more obviously "on their side."[19] In spite of this constraint, however, international actors involved in the SSR process in Sierra Leone—particularly the British—have seen and promoted the ONS as highly successful at what it is called to do, including implementation of reform, coordination of security actors, and analysis of security issues.[20]

The ONS describes itself as a "'clearing house' for the security sector to ensure effective coordination of security and intelligence at national, provincial and district levels—collecting, collating and analyzing intelligence from state security agencies, providing support and secretarial services to the National Security Council."[21] The ONS is further divided into nine functional directorates that deal with (1) Serious Organise Crime Coordination, (2) Protective and Private Security, (3) Research and Assessments, (4) Provincial and Border Security, (5) Finance and Corporate Services, (6) Planning and Inter Agency Relations, (7) Human Resources Management, (8) Disaster Management, and (9) Strategic Communications.[22] The NSC system of Sierra Leone is also decentralized, allowing more direct input from citizens into the national security process. At the subnational level, there exist provincial and district security committees (PROSECs and DISECs) for each province and district of the country, whose structures mirror that of the NSC and which are tasked with carrying out the orders of the NSC.[23] The ONS has local offices at these same administrative levels, which function as secretariats to the PROSECs and DISECs just as the national headquarters ONS itself functions as a secretariat to the NSC.

In terms of finance, Section 32 of Part VIII of the NaSCIA states that "the administrative expenses of the Council and the commit-

---

[19] Interview with subject matter expert, January 22, 2018.

[20] Interview with subject matter expert, January 22, 2018.

[21] Republic of Sierra Leone, The Office of National Security, "About Us," 2017a.

[22] Republic of Sierra Leone, "Directorates," 2017b.

[23] "The National Security and Central Intelligence Act, 2002," pp. 5–7.

tees of the Council . . . shall be a charge on the consolidated fund."[24] This creates an official source of funding for the NSC, thereby providing it with the resources needed to carry out its functions properly. Indeed, the "Appropriations Act, 2002," passed several months ahead of the passage of the NaSCIA, allocated to the "national security adviser" an initial budget of 3.13 million leones, presumably to be used for the NSC and relevant subagencies such as the ONS. For comparison, in the same "Appropriations Act," the Ministry of Internal Affairs received 2.01 million leones, the Cabinet Secretariat 3.29 million leones, the Ministry of Defence 6.83 million leones, the Ministry of Foreign Affairs and International Co-operation 1.54 billion leones, the police 11.8 billion leones, and the military 36.1 billion leones.[25] In U.S. dollar terms, on June 30, 2002, the exchange rate was 2,050 leones to the U.S. dollar.[26] This meant that the NSC had an initial budget of U.S. $1,526.83, compared to the police and the military, which respectively had budgets worth U.S. $5.76 million and U.S. $17.61 million. This placed the NSC at the lower end of the spectrum in terms of budget size. The ONS also previously received funding through a British-led project on SSR in Sierra Leone, but that ended with the project around 2010. The budget for the ONS subsequently was then subsumed into other parts of the central government's budget.[27]

Sierra Leone's National Security Council Within the Framework

Sierra Leone's NSC has positive scores in all seven categories of variables, making it a potential model to follow for overcoming different kinds of potential challenges (see Table 3.1). The Sierra Leone NSC

---

[24] "The National Security and Central Intelligence Act, 2002," p. 8.

[25] "Appropriations Act, 2002," *Sierra Leone Gazette*, Vol. CXXXIII, No. 21, April 18, 2002 (Sierre Leone).

[26] U.S. Department of the Treasury, *Treasury Reporting Rates of Exchange: As of June 30, 2002*, Washington, D.C.: U.S. Government Printing Office, June 30, 2002, p. 4.

[27] Interview with subject matter expert, January 19, 2018.

Table 3.1
Application of Framework to the Case of Sierra Leone

Category	Variable	Level in Present Case
Defining roles and authority	Is there a legislative or constitutional basis for the NSC?	Yes: the NSC is formally established in law with the NaSCIA.
	Does the NSC have the backing of the country's chief executive (head of state or head of government)?	Yes: the president personally chairs the NSC, with the vice president acting as deputy chairman.
Composition and accountability	Is the NSC predominantly civilian but with relevant input from noncivilians?	Yes: the balance tips in favor of civilians (8) vs. noncivilians (3).
	Is the NSC appropriately sized, with virtually all NSC members having national security responsibilities?	Yes: the NSC consists of only 11 statutory members, the majority of whom have responsibilities that deal with some aspect of national security.
	Is there accountability for the NSC?	Yes: appointment of the National Security Coordinator is subject to parliamentary approval, while the CISU must prepare annual reports on its operations.
Ensuring sufficient resources	Does the NSC and its secretariat have appropriate levels of personnel and funding?	Yes: The ONS is composed of between 150 and 200 personnel. Funding for the NSC, and the ONS by extension, is written into law as part of the NaSCIA and is on the low side, far behind the major security actors like the MoD, army, and police. However, this appears to still be sufficient for the ONS to carry out its functions properly. The ONS also has its local offices as well as the PROSECs and DISECs to help carry out the work of the NSC.
	Does the NSC have access to a broad range of expertise?	Yes: the NSC is supported by the ONS, CISU, the JIC, and the PROSECs/DISECs. The president also has the option of inviting others to attend NSC meetings when he considers necessary.

has both a legally defined role and strong authority due to involvement from the highest levels of government. Its composition also tilts in favor of civilian participants while also including relevant noncivilian actors as members. The NSC is compact, consisting of just 11 statutory members. Given that the position of minister of presidential affairs no longer exists, the NSC may now actually consist of just ten statutory members. This allows the NSC to be a nimble forum for top-level discussion and decisionmaking on security issues. It is also politically accountable not only because the appointment of the National Security Coordinator is subject to parliamentary approval but also because the CISU must make annual reports on its operations.

The NSC also has good actual and potential access to a range of expertise. Funding to it and the ONS is an issue. At its creation, the budget given to the NSC was above that given to the Ministry of Internal Affairs but far less than what was given to other major ministries. It also received additional funding from international donors, but this source of funding ended by 2010. This may have had an impact on the ONS's ability to carry out its functions properly, but the lack of publicly available audit reports makes this difficult to determine. However, outside observers, including foreign advisers to the Sierra Leonean government, have informally and qualitatively assessed the ONS to have been highly successful at carrying out its responsibilities.

CHAPTER FOUR

Case Study 2: Côte d'Ivoire

Political Situation of Côte d'Ivoire

Since the early 2000s, Côte d'Ivoire has experienced two major periods of instability—the civil war of 2002 to 2007 and the political crisis of 2010 to 2011.

The civil war began on September 19, 2002, with an attempted coup, which was quickly put down by progovernment forces. Reprisals took place thereafter, during which former president Robert Gueï, "believed to have been behind the coup[,] . . . [was] assassinated under unexplained circumstances along with the Minister of the Interior Émile Boga Doudou."[1] Rebel forces thereafter took control of the northern part of the country, with one of their leaders—Guillaume Soro—demanding that President Laurent Gbagbo step down.[2] France began intervening in the conflict as well; the country launched Operation Licorne on September 22, working to maintain a buffer zone between the north and the south of the country, and, in January 2003, they attempted to implement the Marcoussis Accord, which would have allowed Gbagbo to remain in power while also bringing rebel leaders into the government.[3] However, fighting continued

---

[1] Matthieu Kairouz, "Ce jour-là: le 19 septembre 2002, une tentative de coup d'État ébranle profondément la Côte d'Ivoire" [On That Day: September 19, 2002, an Attempted Coup d'Etat Profoundly Shakes Côte d'Ivoire], *Jeune Afrique*, September 19, 2016.

[2] Radio France Internationale (RFI), "Côte d'Ivoire," November 2017; Kairouz, 2016.

[3] RFI, 2017; Kairouz, 2016.

until March 2007, when the two sides signed the Ouagadougou Accord.[4] In the same month, rebel leader Guillaume Soro was named prime minister, while a ceremony for the "flame of peace" officially ended the war in July of the same year.[5] According to government and media estimates, over 4,000 people were killed in this conflict.[6]

The second period of instability began in 2010, in the aftermath of a contested presidential election between incumbent President Laurent Gbagbo and opposition candidate Alassane Ouattara. After a second round of voting, the Independent Electoral Commission declared Ouattara to be the winner in December 2010. The Constitutional Court, however, invalidated these results, declaring Gbagbo winner, and Gbagbo refused to step down.[7] Pro-Ouattara and pro-Gbagbo forces engaged in conflict for roughly four months afterward, with the United Nations sending 2,000 peacekeepers to the country in January 2011, and with Operation Licorne also intervening.[8] The war officially came to an end in April 2011 with the arrest of Gbagbo and his wife Simone and with the army swearing allegiance to Ouattara.[9] According to International Criminal Court prosecutors, "about 3,000 people died in violence by both sides."[10]

In January 2015, France's Operation Licorne officially came to an end and was replaced by the French Forces in Côte d'Ivoire, with total number of troops increasing from 500 to 900 in 2016.[11] In spite

---

[4]   Kairouz, 2016.

[5]   "Côte d'Ivoire: Chronologie" [Côte d'Ivoire: Timeline], *Jeune Afrique*, updated November 10, 2017.

[6]   Project Ploughshares, *Armed Conflicts Report: Côte d'Ivoire (2002—First Combat Deaths)*, Waterloo, Ont.: Project Ploughshares, updated January 2009.

[7]   "Côte d'Ivoire: Chronologie" [Côte d'Ivoire: Timeline], 2017.

[8]   "Côte d'Ivoire: Chronologie" [Côte d'Ivoire: Timeline], 2017; Agence France-Press, "Côte d'Ivoire: la force française Licorne prend le contrôle de l'aéroport d'Abidjan" [French force Licorne takes control of the Abidjan airport], *Jeune Afrique*, April 3, 2011.

[9]   "Côte d'Ivoire: Chronologie" [Côte d'Ivoire: Timeline], 2017.

[10]   "Ivory Coast: Gbagbo Faces Murder and Rape Charges," *BBC News*, November 30, 2011.

[11]   Agence France-Press, "Côte d'Ivoire: la France annonce l'augmentation de sa présence militaire" [Côte d'Ivoire: France announces increase in its military presence], *Jeune Afrique*, April 29, 2016.

of the end of the civil war and the continued French military presence, however, instability persists in the country. As of May 2017, the government has faced four military mutinies in three years by soldiers demanding increases in their pay. The mutineers are former rebels that had been part of the New Forces (*Forces nouvelles*) and had supported Ouattara during the political crisis of 2010–2011 before becoming integrated into the regular army in 2011.[12]

Côte d'Ivoire's National Security Council

Côte d'Ivoire's NSC originally came into existence with Presidential Decrees No. 96 PR.06 and No. 96 PR.07, both of which were enacted on July 25, 1996. A further decree enacted on August 9 (No. 96 PR.09) nominated Division General Ehuéni Joseph to the position of secretary general of the NSC.[13] This initial NSC was subsequently modified several times by decree.[14] On August 8, 2012, a year after the end of the political crisis, Presidential Decree No. 2012–786 on the "creation, duties, organization and functioning of the National Security Council" came into effect.[15] This created what French researcher Aline Leboeuf describes as a "new type of National Security Council" resembling both the Office of National Security of Sierra Leone and the U.S. National Security Council. It is an "instrument of civil control over the security sector" that "brings together political decision-makers and high-level administrative, civil and military leader," thereby allow-

---

[12] Anna Sylvestre-Treiner and Vincent Duhem, "Côte d'Ivoire: retour sur une étrange mutinerie" [Côte d'Ivoire: Coming Back to a Strange Mutiny], *Jeune Afrique*, May 26, 2017.

[13] Republic of Côte d'Ivoire, "Sommaire" [Summary], *Journal Officiel de la République de Côte d'Ivoire*, No. 34, August 22, 1996.

[14] Aline Leboeuf, *La Réforme du Secteur de Sécurité à l'Ivoirienne [Ivorian Style Security Sector Reform]*, Paris, France: Institut Français des Relations Internationales, March 2016, p. 8fn10.

[15] Republic of Côte d'Ivoire, "Sommaire" [Summary], *Journal Officiel de la République de Côte d'Ivoire*, No. 41, October 11, 2012.

ing "better cooperation and coordination and better implementation of presidential decisions."[16]

The Ivorian NSC has five overall missions, which include (1) coordinating on internal and external security matters; (2) defining strategic direction and deciding on national priorities in security sector reform; (3) providing intelligence to and informing and advising the head of state on security issues; (4) anticipating and managing actions and situations that may threaten the vital interests of the country; and (5) ensuring coordination of activities by different ministries in the security domain and supervising the national intelligence system.[17] At its creation, the NSC consisted of 19 members, including the president; the prime minister, who also serves as minister of justice; the minister of the interior; the minister of foreign affairs; the secretary general of the presidency; the director of the president's personal office;[18] the minister of presidential affairs; the vice minister of defense, attached to the presidency; the minister of the economy and finance; the vice minister of justice, attached to the prime minister; the chief of the president's personal military staff; the head of the president's personal office; the chief of staff of the armed forces; the head of superior commander of the national gendarmerie; the director general of the national police; the commander of the presidential security group; the national intelligence coordinator; the president's defense and security counselor; and the secretary general of the NSC.[19] The NSC meets twice a month, with the president chairing the meetings.[20]

---

[16] Leboeuf, 2016, p. 8.

[17] Republic of Côte d'Ivoire, National Security Council, "Le communiqué du Conseil national de sécurité lu par son secrétaire, Alain Richard Donwahi" [The communique of the national secretary council, as read by its secretary, Alain Richard Donwahi], *Abidjan.net*, August 29, 2012.

[18] The previously cited communique only notes the individual's title as "Monsieur le Ministre, Directeur de cabinet" without specifying further. However, Leboeuf, 2016, p. 8, indicates that the "directeur" is the director of the presidential office, working alongside the "chef de Cabinet."

[19] Republic of Côte d'Ivoire, NSC, 2012.

[20] Kouakou, "ADO a présidé le premier Conseil de National de Sécurité de son nouveau mandat" [ADO Chairs the First National Security Council of His New Term], *Burkina 24*,

Supporting the NSC is a secretariat led by the secretary-general of the NSC. The secretariat is comprised of around 10–20 people and includes experts from France, the United States, and from Côte d'Ivoire itself. One member of the staff, for example, is a Ivorian professor recognized for his expertise on security issues.[21] The secretariat is responsible for: (1) organizing meetings of the NSC; (2) drafting its decision; (3) ensure the implementation of NSC decisions and security sector reforms; and (4) organizing a working group on security sector reforms that meets once per month and that brings together the main national and international actors on this topic.[22] Beyond that, the secretariat has also made outreach efforts to "civil society, NGOs, media, parliamentarians and local administration" in order to get actors in these areas more involved in security sector reforms.[23] It has, for example, organized seminars to "provide members of civil society organizations . . . including representatives of the media, as well as members of the security forces with the necessary tools to become active actors in the implementation of Security Sector Reform" with the support of the United Nations Operation in Côte d'Ivoire (UNOCI).[24] The secretariat of the NSC has coordinated monthly meetings among U.N. donors to Côte d'Ivoire, and under the previous secretary-general Alain Richard Donwahi, the NSC (rather than the Ministry of Defense) was responsible for handling military contracts.[25] Following Donwahi's appointment as minister of defense, the secretariat became relatively less important, as his successor as secretary-general of the NSC has had less personal influence with President Alassane Ouattara.[26]

November 6, 2015.

[21] Interview with subject matter expert, January 23, 2018.

[22] Leboeuf, 2016, p. 9.

[23] Leboeuf, 2016, pp. 16–17.

[24] United Nations, "Security Sector Reform: National Security Council and UNOCI Sensitise Civil Society and Security Forces in Daloa," *UNOCI News*, September 18, 2013.

[25] Interview with subject matter expert, January 23, 2018.

[26] Interview with subject matter expert, January 23, 2018.

Côte d'Ivoire's National Security Council Within the Framework

Information regarding certain aspects of Côte d'Ivoire's NSC is not publicly available, so there are certain variables which this report cannot assess. For example, information regarding the NSC's funding and whether and/or how it is accountable was not found in open sources. Overall, Ivorian NSC is effective in three categories, ineffective in one, and mixed in another two; one category could not be assessed (see Table 4.1). This means that the Ivorian NSC was effective in only three out of seven categories.

The NSC does have legal legitimacy and authority that comes from high-level backing. Its composition also tips in favor of civilians versus noncivilians. On the other hand, the Ivorian NSC is large and includes a number of members who do not have any obvious need to be part of this body. These include both civilian ministers and military commanders who are attached either to the presidency or to the president personally. The number of other noncivilian members may further be reduced, for example, by having the minister of the interior represent the views of both the gendarmerie and the national police, with the commanders of these two forces only being invited to attend on an ad hoc basis. This will help to channel the views of the various security agencies better while also trimming down the NSC to make it a nimbler deliberative and decisionmaking body. Information regarding the NSC's accountability was unavailable. The secretariat, with just a staff of 12, may also not be sufficient to support the NSC and may benefit from having its size and funding expanded.

Table 4.1
Application of Framework to the Case of Côte d'Ivoire

Category	Variable	Level in Present Case
Defining roles and authority	Is there a legislative or constitutional basis for the NSC?	Yes: the NSC is formally established in law with Presidential Decree No. 2012–786.
	Does the NSC have the backing of the country's chief executive (head of state or head of government)?	Yes: the president personally chairs the NSC, while the prime minister is also a member.
Composition and accountability	Is the NSC predominantly civilian but with relevant input from noncivilians?	Yes: the balance tips in favor of civilians (12) vs. noncivilians (7).
	Is the NSC appropriately sized, with virtually all NSC members having national security responsibilities?	No: at least four civilians—the ones responsible for some aspects of the presidency or the president's personal office—have no obvious need to be statutory members of the NSC. At least two noncivilians—the ones responsible for the president's security detail—also have no obvious need to be statutory members of the NSC.
	Is there meaningful accountability for the NSC?	Information unavailable
Ensuring sufficient resources	Does the NSC and its secretariat have appropriate levels of personnel and funding?	Mixed: budgetary figures for the secretariat are unknown. The secretariat consists of just 12 people but does bring in outside expertise.
	Does the NSC have access to a broad range of expertise?	Mixed: the NSC has a small secretariat of 12 people but also brings together outside experts.

CHAPTER FIVE

Case Study 3: Mozambique

Political Situation of Mozambique

In the postwar period, Mozambique has experienced two major periods of upheaval and has more recently seen a return to instability. These include the War of Independence (1964–1975), the Civil War (1976–1992), and the ongoing low-level conflict between the ruling party Frente de Libertação de Moçambique (FRELIMO) and the main opposition Resistência Nacional Moçambicana (RENAMO) (from about 2013 to the present).

For a roughly ten-year period, Mozambique was engaged in a war for independence from the colonial power Portugal, then under the authoritarian Estado Novo of Prime Minister António de Oliveira Salazar. The war began in September 1964, when opposition movement FRELIMO—formed two years earlier in neighboring Tanzania by activists—launched an attack in Chai, an administrative post in Cabo Delgado, Mozambique's northernmost province.[1] Events took a turn in 1974, when a military coup in Portugal led to a democratic transition—afterward known as the Carnation Revolution. In the same year, the new Portuguese government, supporting autonomy for the colonies, signed the Lusaka Accord with FRELIMO, leading

---

[1] "Mozambique Profile—Timeline," *BBC News*, November 2, 2017; Madalena Sampaio, "Cronologia 1961–1969: Início da Guerra Colonial e viragem no destino das colónias" [1961–1969 Timeline: Beginning of the Colonial War and Turning Point in the Destiny of the Colonies], *Deutsche Welle*, December 10, 2013a.

to the establishment of a transitional government in Mozambique.[2] Mozambique became fully independent on June 25, 1975.[3] According to unofficial estimates, the war for independence resulted in a total of 50,000 civilians killed.[4] In the immediate aftermath of the war, 250,000 more Portuguese inhabitants departed from Mozambique.[5]

A year later, in 1976, a civil war began between the ruling FRELIMO—which had established a Marxist-Leninist one-party state—and the opposition RENAMO—which was supported by Rhodesia, apartheid South Africa, and, indirectly, the United States.[6] The war took a turn in 1989, when the Cold War ended. FRELIMO lost its main source of support—the Soviet Union—while RENAMO also lost its support from Zimbabwe and South Africa. The two parties signed a peace treaty in Rome on October 4, 1992.[7] The civil war devastated the country, leading to a million deaths and creating more than 3 million refugees.[8]

Even after the signing of the accords, stability has not entirely returned to Mozambique. "A force of about 300 Renamo men have remained armed since the accord, despite efforts to integrate them into the army or police force."[9] More recently, since June 2013, there has been renewed conflict between FRELIMO and RENAMO.[10] In

---

[2]   "Mozambique Profile—Timeline," 2017.

[3]   Madalena Sampaio, "Cronologia 1974–2002: Das independências ao fim da guerra em Moçambique e Angola" [1974–2002 Timeline: From Independence to the End of War in Mozambique and Angola], *Deutsche Welle*, December 11, 2013b.

[4]   World Peace Foundation, "Mozambique: War of Independence," *Mass Atrocity Endings*, August 7, 2015a.

[5]   "Mozambique Profile—Timeline," 2017.

[6]   Alfredo Lituri, "Cronologia 16 anos de guerra e 20 anos de paz em Moçambique" [Timeline of 16 Years of War and 20 Years of Peace in Mozambique], *SapoNotícias*, October 4, 2012.

[7]   Lituri, 2012.

[8]   Lituri, 2012.

[9]   "Mozambique's RENAMO Ex-Rebels Blamed for Deadly Attacks," *BBC News*, June 21, 2013.

[10]   "Mozambique's RENAMO Ex-Rebels Blamed for Deadly Attacks," 2013.

October of the same year, RENAMO announced that it was abandoning the 1992 peace accord with FRELIMO.[11] In consequence, from mid-2015 to early 2016, "12,000 Mozambicans [had] fled to neighboring Malawi."[12] As of November 2017, peace talks between FRELIMO and RENAMO continue, with the two sides working to finalize documents on decentralization in order to sign a peace accord, which will then go to parliament.[13]

Mozambique's National Security Council

Mozambique's National Defense and Security Council (CNDS) was created by Law No. 8/96 on July 5, 1996, with the original intent that it would serve as a "consultative organ to the Head of State on matters related to national sovereignty, territorial integrity, defense and security."[14] The existence of the CNDS is further incorporated into the country's 2004 constitution under Chapter II, Title XIII. On October 3, 2017, Mozambique's government further submitted a bill to the Assembly of the Republic that would make changes to the CNDS that would, according to the official communique, "adjust the legal framework that regulates the organization, composition and functioning of the National Defense and Security Council, conforming it to the Constitution of the Republic."[15] Government spokesperson Ana

---

[11] Manuel Mucari, "Mozambique Faces Uncertainty as Renamo Ends 1992 Peace Pact," *Reuters*, October 21, 2013.

[12] Tom Bowker, Simon Kamm, and Aurelio Sambo, "Mozambique's Invisible Civil War," *Foreign Policy*, May 6, 2016.

[13] "'Iremos nos encontrar em breve' Dhlakama," ["We will meet soon" Dhlakama], *Folha De Maputo*, November 6, 2017.

[14] "Chefe do Estado nomeia membros do Conselho de Defesa e Segurança," [Head of State Nominates Members of the Defense and Security Council], *Jornal Noticias*, August 11, 2015; "Conselho de Defesa e Segurança pede calma ao moçambicanos, após onda de tumultos," [Defense and Security Council Asks for Calm from Mozambicans After Wave of Unrest], *Diário de Notícias*, October 26, 2017.

[15] Republic of Mozambique, "Comunicado da 34 Sessão Ordinária do Conselho de Ministros" [Communique of the 34th Ordinary Session of the Council of Ministers], *Comunicados*

Comoana specified that the proposed adjustments clarify the legal status of the CNDS and clarify such topics as length of terms and immunity for its members.[16]

According to Article 268 of the 2004 constitution, "the National Defense and Security Council is presided over by the President of the Republic, with its composition determined by law, including two members designated by the President of the Republic and five by the Assembly of the Republic."[17] In practice, the CNDS is much larger, and, as of October 2017, it consists of 20 members, including the president; prime minister; president of the Assembly of the Republic; the ministers of national defense, the interior, foreign affairs and cooperation, economy and finance, transport and communications, justice, and constitutional and religious affairs; the director-general of the State Information and Security Service; the chief of staff of the Armed Defense Forces of Mozambique; the commandant-general of the Republic of Mozambique Police; two additional members designated by the president; and five additional members elected by the Assembly of the Republic, three by the FRELIMO parliamentary bench, and two by the RENAMO parliamentary bench.[18] The Mozambican government has also considered further expanding its membership to include ministers whose portfolios touch on national sovereignty in some way, such as the Minister of the Sea, Inland Waters, and Fisheries.[19]

Article 269 of the 2004 constitution lists the specific powers of the CNDS. These include the ability to: make preliminary decisions on the declaration of war; decide on the suspension of constitutional guarantees and declare a state of siege or state of emergency; give advice

---

2017, Secretariat of the Council of Ministers, Republic of Mozambique, October 3, 2017.

[16] "Governo altera funcionamento do conselho de defesa e segurança," [Government Changes Functioning of Defense and Security Council], *Folha de Maputo*, October 4, 2017.

[17] Republic of Mozambique, *Constituição da República* [*Constitution of the Republic*], Government of Mozambique, 2004, p. 86.

[18] "Governo altera funcionamento do conselho de defesa e segurança," 2017.

[19] "Governo moçambicano revê regulamento do Conselho Nacional de Defesa," [Mozambican Government Reviews Regulation of National Defense Council], *Diário de Notícias*, October 3, 2017.

on the criteria and conditions for using total or partial protection zones for the purposes of the defense and security of national territory; and analyze and assist with initiatives of other state organs that are intended to guarantee the consolidation of national independence, the reinforcement of democratic political power, and the maintaining of law and order.[20] In addition, the CNDS has a secretariat. Little public information is available regarding this body, but it works with the president's military staff (*Casa Militar*) to prepare meetings of the CNDS as well as to carry out other activities.[21]

Mozambique's National Security Council Within the Framework

Similar to the case of Côte d'Ivoire, information regarding the finances of Mozambique's NSC could not be found in open sources. The Mozambique NSC, therefore, could not be assessed in this category. Overall, Mozambique's NSC is effective in four categories, ineffective in one, and mixed in another two—meaning that it is effective in four out of seven categories (see Table 5.1).

Mozambique's NSC has significant legitimacy, derived not only from law but also from being incorporated directly into the constitution. The president, meanwhile, is its chairman. In terms of its composition, the balance tips in favor of civilians. Among the 13 members who are identified by title, ten are civilians, while only three are noncivilians. The remaining two members designated by the president and remaining five members elected by the Assembly of the Republic may be either civilian or noncivilian, but even if all seven of them were noncivilian, there would still be an equal balance of civilian and noncivilian members of the NSC. However, the NSC overall seem to be too large, with what appears to be an attempt by the government to represent all possible interests. At least two ministers—transport and the sea—do not

---

[20] Republic of Mozambique, 2004, p. 86.

[21] Republic of Mozambique, "Casa Militar" [Military House], Presidency of the Republic of Mozambique [Presidência da República de Moçambique], n.d.

Table 5.1
Application of Framework to the Case of Mozambique

Category	Variable	Level in Present Case
Defining roles and authority	Is there a legislative or constitutional basis for the NSC?	Yes: the NSC is formally established in both law and the constitution.
	Does the NSC have the backing of the country's chief executive (head of state or head of government)?	Yes: the president personally chairs the NSC, while the prime minister is also a member.
Composition and accountability	Is the NSC predominantly civilian but with relevant input from noncivilians?	Yes: in terms of defined members, the balance tips in favor of civilians (10) vs. noncivilians (3). The status of the two additional members designated by the president and the five additional members elected by parliament are unknown.
	Is the NSC appropriately sized, with virtually all NSC members having national security responsibilities?	No: at least two of the ministers—transport and sea—do not need to be statutory members of the NSC. Similarly, the seven additional, nominated members do not need to be statutory members but could be invited to attend meetings on an ad hoc basis.
	Is there accountability for the NSC?	Mixed: the president of parliament and two representatives of the opposition RENAMO sit on the NSC, but how much accountability this creates is unknown.
Ensure sufficient resources	Does the NSC and its secretariat have appropriate levels of personnel and funding?	Mixed: information regarding the size and finances of the secretariat was unavailable, but it does work alongside the president's military staff, suggesting that it can draw on other resources to help it carry out its functions.
	Does the NSC have access to a broad range of expertise?	Yes: the NSC has seven additional members that the president and parliament may designate. This may help it bring in outside expertise.

need to be statutory members of the NSC. While transportation and the administration of natural resources may be important nontraditional security issues, governments around the world have usually not considered them to have direct implications on national security—as evidenced by the composition of NSCs in countries such as France, Japan, Turkey, the United States, the United Kingdom, and others. The additional members chosen by the president and the Assembly of the Republic also do not need to be statutory members of the NSC and could instead simply be invited to attend and provide their expertise only when needed. Removing them would help to trim the NSC down to just 13 members. In terms of accountability, the NSC includes both the president of the Assembly of the Republic and two members nominated by the opposition RENAMO. How much that increases accountability, though, is debatable, as the president of the Assembly also belongs to the governing FRELIMO, while the RENAMO-nominated members are completely outnumbered.

In terms of financing, information regarding the NSC and its secretariat is unavailable. The secretariat may be able to call on other agencies, such as the president's military staff, to help it carry out its tasks. The degree to which the NSC has access to a broad range of expertise is also unknown. At least within the NSC itself, it may benefit from the insight of the seven additional members, depending on their background. However, if these seven were removed from the NSC as part of an effort to reduce its size, the NSC may no longer be able to access their expertise as regularly as before.

CHAPTER SIX

Conclusion

The objectives of this report were to look at the potential challenges that may arise from establishing an NSC and then to create a framework for systematically assessing how to effectively overcome such challenges—so as to provide the government of Mali with a reference as it examines how to establish such an NSC for itself. The report's overall approach was twofold: (1) a review of preexisting literature and other open sources that was then used to build a theoretical framework and then (2) an application of this framework to a series of case studies. The sources used for the review include studies on NSCs as a general topic, on individual NSCs, on SSR as a general topic, and on SSR in individual countries, as well as interviews with subject matter experts. Keeping in mind that NSCs may differ radically from each other as a function of their environments, this report took the most commonly cited critiques and recommendations on how best to shape NSCs—while also making inferences where necessary. It then matches up this information against the various categories of potential challenges that might arise from setting up an NSC in order to see what specific features help to overcome such challenges. Together, these elements constitute the framework.

In terms of case studies, this report looked at Sierra Leone, Côte d'Ivoire, and Mozambique. These three countries may be of particular relevance to Mali, given the similarity of their environments and historical experiences of political/military instability. These similarities help to control for "confounding variables" as far as possible in the application of the framework. Additionally, there was more widely available information regarding these countries' NSCs than was the case for other countries' NSCs. That being said, there were still information gaps regarding the examined countries' NSCs. This was particularly the case when it came to the NSCs' support agencies and streams of funding, for which information was mostly unavailable. If such information had been available, that may have changed some of the preceding analysis. In general, the usefulness of the framework depends to a large extent on availability of information. The greater the amount of information supplied, the more complete and thorough the analysis.

Having an NSC could be a major advantage for a government, particularly in terms of providing it with a top-level body for implementing security sector reforms or responding to contingencies in a timelier, more coordinated manner. A number of challenges may arise from setting up a new NSC, however. These challenges fall into three overall categories: (1) the NSC becomes overly powerful, gradually usurping the authority of preexisting agencies and transforming into an additional layer of bureaucracy; (2) the NSC becomes a tool for authoritarian consolidation, concentrating control over the country's security forces and working in a partisan manner against the government's political opponents; and (3) the NSC drains and/or steals resources away from other agencies, gradually hollowing them out.

As this report has argued, the elements to overcoming these challenges and to creating an effective NSC fall into three categories overall: (1) definition of role and authority, (2) composition and accountability, and (3) sufficient resources. Defining the role of the NSC, particularly through law, can help cement its legitimacy and prevent it from overreaching. Authority, meanwhile, comes from top-level backing from the country's chief executive. The NSC's composition is important in that it should be composed of a wide enough range of actors to be able to act effectively as a whole-of-government forum for discussing strategic issues. At the same time, it should not be a bloated body that includes statutory members who do not have any obvious need to be part of the NSC and therefore merely attend in order to represent particular interests. It should further not be composed primarily of military and security personnel and should also be accountable in some way in

order to prevent the NSC from becoming a tool for authoritarian consolidation. Ensuring adequate resources—both material such as funding and nonmaterial such as expertise—allows the NSC to be informed
and effectively carry out its functions. Clearly defined resource streams
also help to mitigate draining of resources away from other agencies.

The specific NSCs examined in the case studies—Sierra Leone,
Côte d'Ivoire, and Mozambique—did well in the first category, both
having legal existence and being chaired personally by the country's
president. Additionally, Sierra Leone did well in the second category,
being predominantly civilian—but with appropriate input from noncivilians—while also not being overly large. While the other two
countries did well in terms of their balance of civilian versus noncivilian members, they also had a number of superfluous civilian and noncivilian members who did not need to be part of the NSC. Removing
these superfluous members would still leave the two countries' NSCs
with predominantly civilian memberships. Sierra Leone also appeared
to do the best in terms of accountability, given that its national security coordinator had to be approved by parliament, while a subordinate agency of the NSC also had to present annual reports to parliament. Information for Côte d'Ivoire was unavailable, while in the case
of Mozambique, there appeared to only be informal accountability by
including opposition-nominated representatives and the president of
the parliament as members of the NSC. For the third category of variables, it was more difficult to assess the three countries, as there was
less information available. The Sierra Leone NSC appeared to have
also done the best in these categories. Its budget is relatively limited,
particularly after 2010 when foreign donor funding ended, and its
action arm—the ONS—is compact, consisting of between 150 and
200 staff. However, in spite these limitations, experts and other outside observers have seen the ONS as being competent and a major success within the overall SSR process in Sierra Leone. The NSC has also
benefited from its devolved structure—with provincial and district
security committees (PROSECs and DISECs)—which bring together
relevant actors to discuss and handle security issues at different levels
of government. This provides the NSC, with its relatively limited
resources, with a broader network of people to help carry out its mis-

sion. At the same time, it serves as a guard against the NSC being used as a tool for authoritarian consolidation. This devolved structure also gives citizens more direct input into security issues and gives greater prominence to local security concerns. Overall, Sierra Leone appears to have been the most successful at overcoming the challenges that arise from creating a new national security decisionmaking structure, making it a potential model to follow for the government of Mali.

Should the government of Mali decide to follow Sierra Leone's path, there are a number of additional points they will have to consider very early on. These include what precise role they envision their new NSC playing and what size support staff they see as being adequate to accomplish that. Sierra Leone decided to create a relatively compact secretariat—the ONS—to support their NSC, going for small but effective. The government of Mali will have to decide whether that is suitable for their needs. Sierra Leone also decided on a devolved structure, with the PROSECs and DISECs acting at different levels of government in order to more effectively integrate the country as a whole into the SSR process. With the north of their country still unsettled, the government of Mali will also need to decide if that is a viable approach for them—that is, whether they should set up subnational level security committees or similar structures and whether they should attempt to do so in just the south of the country or in the north as well. Such an approach has its merits, however—particularly in terms of bringing the SSR process closer to the grassroots level. This allows the general public to be more involved and to feel that government authorities are actually listening to their concerns, which in turn allows them to have a greater stake in the success of the process. On the flip side, it allows government authorities to work alongside those who are most directly affected by problems of insecurity, handling issues straight at their source before they have a chance to accumulate and build up to the national level.

Based on the analysis of the three case studies, it is possible to recommend the following options to the government of Mali as it looks to establish its own NSC (see Table 6.1). It should be noted that, in categories where there are multiple options, the options are not mutually exclusive but may be complementary. For example, in terms of having meaningful accountability, the government of Mali could

Table 6.1
National Security Council Options for the Government of Mali

Category	Variable	Option(s)
Defining roles and authority	Is there a legislative or constitutional basis for the NSC?	Establish the NSC through law. Specify in the law what the composition, authorities, sources of funding, and other modalities of the NSC are.
	Does the NSC have the backing of the country's chief executive (head of state or head of government)?	Because of the importance of the NSC and the issues it handles, both the president and the prime minister should be statutory members of the NSC, with the former serving as its chair.
Composition and accountability	Is there a balance between civilian and noncivilian members of the NSC?	There should be a balance of civilian and noncivilian members, although the NSC should be slightly tipped in favor of civilians.
	Is the NSC appropriately sized, with virtually all NSC members having national security responsibilities?	Core members of the NSC should include the ministers for defense, foreign affairs, justice, etc. Military and intelligence chiefs could also serve as advisers. Officials who do not have duties directly related to national security should only be invited to attend when necessary.
	Is there meaningful accountability for the NSC?	1. The national security adviser should be appointed only on parliamentary approval. 2. The NSC should present periodic reports on its activities to parliament. 3. The NSC should consult parliament on major issues such as domestic deployment of the armed forces. 4. The NSC should include representatives from other political parties.
Ensuring sufficient resources	Does the NSC and its secretariat have appropriate levels of personnel and funding?	1. The NSC and its secretariat should have funding streams ensured by legislation and have a formal process for recruiting staff members. 2. The NSC and its secretariat should have a devolved structure with subnational committees to help implement decisions. 3. The NSC and its secretariat should work with other institutions to share the resources and burdens.

Table 6.1—Continued

Category	Variable	Option(s)
	Does the NSC have access to a broad range of expertise?	1. The NSC should draw on expertise across other national agencies and/or across different levels of government. 2. The NSC should draw on outside expertise, such as academia and the private sector.

choose to have the national security adviser's appointment subject to parliamentary approval. Failing that, the NSC could present periodic reports on its activities to parliament or consult parliament on major issues, such as domestic deployment of the armed forces. It may also include representatives from other political parties. It could also choose to implement all of these options together.

To a large degree, how successful an NSC is in overcoming the various potential challenges discussed depends on political will. Moreover, the importance of an NSC capable of overcoming these challenges notwithstanding, it is not a cure-all for general security problems facing a country. Having a well-functioning NSC may not be enough to ensure stability or effective implementation of security sector reform in a postconflict environment. Even if an NSC gets everything "right" on paper, there may still be external elements that continue to contribute to instability. Poverty and the inability to pay for government services and public employees—particularly those in the security sector—are two such elements. This continues to be a concern for Sierra Leone, for example, in spite of its image as a model case of security sector reform. The inability to fully integrate former combatants into the regular armed forces is another factor. Thus, in Côte d'Ivoire, the government continues to face mutinies from certain segments of the armed forces. In Mozambique, meanwhile, the opposition RENAMO has never fully disarmed. RENAMO has representatives on the country's NSC, which should make them feel that they have more of a stake in the governance of the country, but they still retain the option of resorting to the use of force if they ever feel it to be necessary. Constructing an effective NSC is, therefore, an important action for a government—but one which should be undertaken in conjunction with reforms elsewhere.

References

Andersen, Peter, "President Koroma's Fifth Cabinet: 13 March 2016 to 27 March 2018," *The Sierra Leone Web*, 2018. As of August 19, 2018:
http://www.sierra-leone.org/cabinet-koroma5.html

Agence France-Press, "Côte d'Ivoire: la force française Licorne prend le contrôle de l'aéroport d'Abidjan" [French force Licorne takes control of the Abidjan airport], *Jeune Afrique*, April 3, 2011. As of November 18, 2017:
http://www.jeuneafrique.com/154235/politique/c-te-d-ivoire-la-force-fran-aise -licorne-prend-le-contr-le-de-l-a-roport-d-abidjan/

―――, "Côte d'Ivoire: la France annonce l'augmentation de sa présence militaire" [Côte d'Ivoire: France announces increase in its military presence], *Jeune Afrique*, April 29, 2016. As of November 18, 2017:
http://www.jeuneafrique.com/depeches/322042/politique/cote-divoire-france -annonce-laugmentation-de-presence-militaire/

"Appropriations Act, 2002," *Sierra Leone Gazette*, Vol. CXXXIII, No. 21, April 18, 2002. As of November 17, 2017:
http://www.sierra-leone.org/Laws/2002-8.pdf

Bearne, Susanna, Olga Oliker, Kevin A. O'Brien, and Andrew Rathmell, *National Security Decision-Making Structures and Security Sector Reform*, Santa Monica, Calif.: RAND Corporation, TR-289-SSDAT, 2005. As of August 17, 2018:
https://www.rand.org/pubs/technical_reports/TR289.html

Bowker, Tom, Simon Kamm, and Aurelio Sambo, "Mozambique's Invisible Civil War," *Foreign Policy*, May 6, 2016. As of November 18, 2017:
http://foreignpolicy.com/2016/05/06/mozambiques-invisible-civil-war-renamo -frelimo-dhlakama-nyusi/

Cancian, Mark F., "Limiting the Size of NSC Staff," Washington, D.C.: Center for Strategic and International Studies, July 1, 2016. As of January 23, 2018:
https://www.csis.org/analysis/limiting-size-nsc-staff

"Chefe do Estado nomeia membros do Conselho de Defesa e Segurança" [Head of State Nominates Members of the Defense and Security Council], *Jornal Notícias*, August 11, 2015. As of November 16, 2017:
http://www.jornalnoticias.co.mz/index.php/breves/41310-chefe-do-estado-nomeia-membros-do-conselho-de-defesa-e-seguranca.html

Clinton White House Archives, "The National Security Council. Legal Advisor: Special Assistant to the President and Legal Advisor," n.d. As of July 16, 2018:
https://clintonwhitehouse5.archives.gov/WH/EOP/NSC/html/legal.html

"Conselho de Defesa e Segurança pede calma ao moçambicanos, após onda de tumultos" [Defense and Security Council Asks for Calm from Mozambicans After Wave of Unrest], *Diário de Notícias*, October 26, 2017. As of November 26, 2017:
https://www.dn.pt/lusa/interior/conselho-de-defesa-e-seguranca-pede-calma-aos-mocambicanos-apos-onda-de-tumultos-8875450.html

Conteh, Kellie Hassan, "Security Sector Reform in Sierra Leone and the Role of the Office of National Security," in Peter Albrecht and Paul Jackson, eds., *Security Sector Reform in Sierra Leone 1997–2007: Views from the Front Line*, Geneva: Geneva Centre for the Democratic Control of Armed Forces, 2010, pp. 171–182.

"Côte d'Ivoire: Chronologie" [Côte d'Ivoire: Timeline], *Jeune Afrique*, updated November 10, 2017. As of November 18, 2017:
http://www.jeuneafrique.com/pays/cote-divoire/chronologie

DCAF—*See* Geneva Centre for the Democratic Control of Armed Forces.

Dennys, Christian, and Tom Hamilton-Baillie, *Strategic Support to Security Sector Reform in Afghanistan, 2001–2010*, SSR Issue Papers No. 6, Waterloo, Ont.: The Centre for International Governance Innovation, January 2012. As of November 20, 2017:
https://www.cigionline.org/sites/default/files/ssr_issue_no6.pdf

Geneva Centre for the Democratic Control of Armed Forces, "National Security Councils (and Related Bodies)," *DCAF Backgrounder* 11/2010, Geneva, November 2010, pp. 5–6. As of November 17, 2017:
http://www.davidmlaw.com/wp-content/uploads/2012/01/NSCs_2010.pdf

Ghimire, Madhav, "A Case for Redesigning Nepal's National Security Council," *Foreign Policy*, August 13, 2014. As of November 20, 2017:
http://foreignpolicy.com/2014/08/13/a-case-for-redesigning-nepals-national-security-council/

Gompert, David C., Olga Oliker, Brooke Stearns, Keith Crane, and K. Jack Riley, *Making Liberia Safe: Transformation of the National Security Sector*, Santa Monica, Calif.: RAND Corporation, MG-529-OSD, 2007. As of August 17, 2018:
https://www.rand.org/pubs/monographs/MG529.html

"Governo altera funcionamento do conselho de defesa e segurança" [Government Changes Functioning of Defense and Security Council], *Folha de Maputo*, October 4, 2017. As of November 16, 2017:
http://www.folhademaputo.co.mz/pt/noticias/nacional/governo-altera
-funcionamento-do-conselho-de-defesa-e-seguranca/

"Governo moçambicano revê regulamento do Conselho Nacional de Defesa" [Mozambican Government Reviews Regulation of National Defense Council], *Diário de Notícias,* October 3, 2017. As of November 16, 2017:
https://www.dn.pt/lusa/interior/governo-mocambicano-reve-regulamento-do
-conselho-nacional-de-defesa-8817948.html

Human Rights Watch, *The Elephant in the Room: Reforming Zimbabwe's Security Sector Ahead of Elections,* New York: Human Rights Watch, June 4, 2013. As of November 20, 2017:
https://www.hrw.org/report/2013/06/04/elephant-room/reforming-zimbabwes
-security-sector-ahead-elections

"'Iremos nos encontrar em breve' Dhlakama" ["We will meet soon" Dhlakama], *Folha De Maputo*, November 6, 2017. As of November 18, 2017:
http://www.folhademaputo.co.mz/pt/noticias/nacional/iremos-nos-encontrar
-em-breve-dhlakama/

"Ivory Coast: Gbagbo Faces Murder and Rape Charges," *BBC News,* November 30, 2011. As of November 18, 2017:
http://www.bbc.com/news/world-africa-15960254

Kairouz, Matthieu, "Ce jour-là: le 19 septembre 2002, une tentative de coup d'État ébranle profondément la Côte d'Ivoire" [On That Day: September 19, 2002, an Attempted Coup d'Etat Profoundly Shakes Côte d'Ivoire], *Jeune Afrique,* September 19, 2016. As of November 18, 2017:
http://www.jeuneafrique.com/356203/politique/jour-19-septembre-2002-tentative
-de-coup-detat-ebranle-profondement-cote-divoire/

Kaldor, Mary, with James Vincent, *Case Study Sierra Leone: Evaluation of UNDP Assistance to Conflict-Affected Countries*, New York: United Nations Development Programme Evaluation Office, 2006. As of November 18, 2017:
http://web.undp.org/evaluation/documents/thematic/conflict/SierraLeone.pdf

Khalil, Asem, "The Legal Framework for Palestinian Security Sector Governance" in Roland Friedrich and Arnold Luethold, eds., *Entry-Points for Palestinian Security Sector Reform*, Geneva: Geneva Centre for the Democratic Control of Armed Forces, 2007, pp. 31–44. As of November 20, 2017:
http://www.dcaf.ch/sites/default/files/publications/documents/
Entry-Points%28EN%29.pdf

Kouakou, "ADO a présidé le premier Conseil de National de Sécurité de son nouveau mandat" [ADO Chairs the First National Security Council of His New Term], *Burkina 24,* November 6, 2015. As of January 11, 2018: https://burkina24.com/2015/11/06/ado-a-preside-le-premier-conseil-national -de-securite-de-son-nouveau-mandat/

Leboeuf, Aline, *La Réforme du Secteur de Sécurité à l'Ivoirienne* [*Ivorian Style Security Sector Reform*], Paris, France: Institut Français des Relations Internationales, March 2016. As of November 17, 2017: https://www.ifri.org/sites/default/files/atoms/files/etude_progafsub_leboeuf_ok.pdf

Lituri, Alfredo, "Cronologia 16 anos de guerra e 20 anos de paz em Moçambique" [Timeline of 16 Years of War and 20 Years of Peace in Mozambique], *SapoNotícias,* October 4, 2012. As of November 18, 2017: http://noticias.sapo.mz/info/artigo/1273387.html

"Mozambique Profile—Timeline," *BBC News,* November 2, 2017. As of November 18, 2017: http://www.bbc.com/news/world-africa-13890720

"Mozambique's Renamo Ex-Rebels Blamed for Deadly Attacks," *BBC News,* June 21, 2013. As of November 18, 2017: http://www.bbc.com/news/world-africa-23001784

Mucari, Manuel, "Mozambique Faces Uncertainty as Renamo Ends 1992 Peace Pact," *Reuters,* October 21, 2013. As of November 18, 2017: https://www.reuters.com/article/us-mozambique-renamo/mozambique-faces -uncertainty-as-renamo-ends-1992-peace-pact-idUSBRE99K0LI20131021

NaSCIA—*See* "The National Security and Central Intelligence Act, 2002."

"The National Security and Central Intelligence Act, 2002," *Supplement to the Sierra Leone Gazette,* Vol. CXXXII, No. 42, July 4, 2002. As of November 17, 2017: http://www.sierra-leone.org/Laws/2002-10.pdf

ONS—*See* Republic of Sierra Leone, The Office of National Security.

Palestinian Academic Society for the Study of International Affairs and Geneva Centre for the Democratic Control of Armed Forces, "Security Sector Reform in the Palestinian Territories: Challenges and Prospects, Workshop Summary Report" in *Palestinian Security Sector Governance: Challenges and Prospects,* Jerusalem and Geneva, August 2006, pp. 7–30. As of November 20, 2017: https://www.files.ethz.ch/isn/109351/pal_sec_sec_gov_eng.pdf

PASSIA and DCAF—*See* Palestinian Academic Society for the Study of International Affairs and Geneva Centre for the Democratic Control of Armed Forces.

Project Ploughshares, *Armed Conflicts Report: Côte d'Ivoire (2002–First Combat Deaths)*, Waterloo, Ont.: Project Ploughshares, updated January 2009. As of November 18, 2017:
https://www.justice.gov/sites/default/files/eoir/legacy/2014/02/25/Cote_d%27Ivoire.pdf

Radio France Internationale (RFI), "Côte d'Ivoire," November 2017. As of November 18, 2017:
http://www.rfi.fr/contenu/cote-ivoire-chronologie-dates-carte-geographie-demographie-economie-chiffres

Republic of Côte d'Ivoire, "Sommaire" [Summary], *Journal Officiel de la République de Côte d'Ivoire*, No. 34, August 22, 1996. As of November 17, 2017:
http://abidjan.net/JO/JO/2891996.asp

———, "Sommaire" [Summary], *Journal Officiel de la République de Côte d'Ivoire*, No. 41, October 11, 2012. As of November 17, 2017:
http://abidjan.net/JO/JO/12202012.asp

Republic of Côte d'Ivoire, NSC—*See* Republic of Côte d'Ivoire, National Security Council.

Republic of Côte d'Ivoire, National Security Council, "Le communiqué du Conseil national de sécurité lu par son secrétaire, Alain Richard Donwahi" [The communique of the national secretary council, as read by its secretary, Alain Richard Donwahi], *Abidjan.net,* August 29, 2012. As of November 17, 2017:
http://news.abidjan.net/h/439743.html

Republic of Mozambique, "Casa Militar" [Military House], Presidency of the Republic of Mozambique [Presidência da República de Moçambique], n.d. As of November 19, 2017:
http://www.presidencia.gov.mz/por/Presidencia/A-Casa-Militar

———, *Constituição da República* [*Constitution of the Republic*], Government of Mozambique, 2004. As of November 16, 2017:
http://www.portaldogoverno.gov.mz/por/Media/Files/Constituicao-da-Republica-PDF

———, "Comunicado da 34ª Sessão Ordinária do Conselho de Ministros" [Communique of the 34th Ordinary Session of the Council of Ministers], *Comunicados 2017,* Secretariat of the Council of Ministers, Republic of Mozambique, October 3, 2017.

Republic of Sierra Leone, The Office of National Security, "About Us," 2017a. As of November 17, 2017:
http://ons.gov.sl/about-us/

———, "Directorates," 2017b. As of November 17, 2017:
http://ons.gov.sl/departments/

Republic of Sierra Leone, ONS—*See* Republic of Sierra Leone, The Office of National Security.

RFI—*See* Radio France Internationale.

Ries, Charles P., *Improving Decisionmaking in a Turbulent World*, Santa Monica, Calif.: RAND Corporation, PE-192-RC, 2016. As of August 18, 2018: https://www.rand.org/pubs/perspectives/PE192.html

Sampaio, Madalena, "Cronologia 1961–1969: Início da Guerra Colonial e viragem no destino das colónias" [1961–1969 Timeline: Beginning of the Colonial War and Turning Point in the Destiny of the Colonies], *Deutsche Welle,* December 10, 2013a. As of November 18, 2017: https://www.dw.com/pt-002/cronologia-1961-1969-início-da-guerra-colonial -e-viragem-no-destino-das-colónias/a-17280932

———, "Cronologia 1974–2002: Das independências ao fim da guerra em Moçambique e Angola" [1974–2002 Timeline: From Independence to the End of War in Mozambique and Angola], *Deutsche Welle*, December 11, 2013b. As of November 18, 2017: https://www.dw.com/pt-002/cronologia-1974-2002-das-independências-ao-fim -da-guerra-em-moçambique-e-angola/a-17280940

Sécretariat Général de la Défense et de la Sécurité Nationale, *Rapport d'Activité 2015* [*Activity Report 2015*], Paris, France: Sécretariat Général de la Défense et de la Sécurité Nationale, 2015. As of January 24, 2018: http://www.sgdsn.gouv.fr/uploads/2017/01/rapport-d-activite-2015-du-sgdsn.pdf

———, *Rapport d'Activité 2016* [*Activity Report 2016*], Paris, France: Sécretariat Général de la Défense et de la Sécurité Nationale, 2016. As of January 24, 2018: http://www.sgdsn.gouv.fr/uploads/2017/06/rapport-2016-sgdsn-pdf-definition -moyenne.pdf

Sierra Leone Government, *Defence White Paper: Informing the People*, Freetown, SL: Directorate of Defence Policy, Ministry of Defence, 2003. As of July 16, 2018: http://www.mod.gov.sl/docs/MODDefenceWhitePaperSierraLeone.pdf

"Sierra Leone Profile—Timeline," *BBC News,* July 13, 2017. As of November 18, 2017: http://www.bbc.com/news/world-africa-14094419

Sylvestre-Treiner, Anna, and Vincent Duhem, "Côte d'Ivoire: retour sur une étrange mutinerie" [Côte d'Ivoire: Coming Back to a Strange Mutiny], *Jeune Afrique*, May 26, 2017. As of November 18, 2017: http://www.jeuneafrique.com/mag/440562/politique/cote-divoire-retour -mutinerie-reussie/

UNAMSIL—*See* United Nations Mission in Sierra Leone.

United Nations, "Security Sector Reform: National Security Council and UNOCI Sensitise Civil Society and Security Forces in Daloa," *UNOCI News,* September 18, 2013. As of November 19, 2017:
https://onuci.unmissions.org/en/security-sector-reform-national-security-council-and-unoci-sensitise-civil-society-and-security

United Nations Mission in Sierra Leone, "Sierra Leone—UNAMSIL—Facts and Figures," in *The Wayback Machine,* September 12, 2008. As of November 18, 2017:
https://web.archive.org/web/20080912071418/http://www.un.org/Depts/dpko/missions/unamsil/facts.html

U.S. Department of State, Office of the Historian, "History of the National Security Council, 1947–1997," *The Clinton White House Archives,* August 1997. As of January 11, 2018:
https://clintonwhitehouse2.archives.gov/WH/EOP/NSC/html/NSChistory.html#history

U.S. Department of Treasury, *Treasury Reporting Rates of Exchange: As of June 30, 2002,* Washington, D.C.: U.S. Government Printing Office, June 30, 2002. As of July 13, 2018:
https://www.gpo.gov/fdsys/pkg/GOVPUB-T63_100-fab63240b6208a926bd391a4d87ad4e2/pdf/GOVPUB-T63_100-fab63240b6208a926bd391a4d87ad4e2.pdf

World Peace Foundation, "Mozambique: War of Independence," *Mass Atrocity Endings*, August 7, 2015a. As of November 18, 2017:
https://sites.tufts.edu/atrocityendings/2015/08/07/mozambique-war-of-independence/

———, "Sierra Leone," *Mass Atrocity Endings*, August 7, 2015b. As of November 18, 2017:
https://sites.tufts.edu/atrocityendings/2015/08/07/sierra-leone/